CAMPBELTOWN

IN DAYS GONE BY

Carol McNeill

First published 2009

ISBN 978-0-9534686-3-8

Published by
Fife Publicity
fifepublicity@ukonline.co.uk
www.carolmcneill.co.uk

Printed by
Multiprint (Scotland) Limited, Kirkcaldy
Telephone 01592 204755
www.multiprint.tv

Acknowledgements:

Many thanks to Argyll and Bute Library Service for their kind
permission to use a selection of the MacGrory Collection of images,
and in particular to Eleanor Harris, Local Studies Librarian.
Grateful thanks also to Eileen Baird and Angus Martin for all their
help and information, and to Jim Swan for cover design.

Introduction

Getting a glimpse of what Campbeltown looked like in the early 1900s is all thanks to two brothers, Charles and Dennis MacGrory, who indulged their passion of photography and left us an invaluable legacy: images of people, buildings, landscapes and a whole way of life which have all long since disappeared.

The MacGrory brothers, born in Campbeltown in the 1860s, originally opened a pawnbroker's shop which developed into a large draper's and outfitter's on the corner of Main Street and Bolgam Street. In their spare time in the years between roughly 1890 and 1914, they photographed every aspect of local life. They used the heavy plate cameras and photographic equipment of the time – no mean feat before the days of digital cameras – to capture images not only in Campbeltown and other parts of Kintyre, but also on their travels to Iona and elsewhere in Scotland, Ireland and the Continent.

They had a gift for recording contemporary images, and the people who came under the scrutiny of their camera lens seemed to have been remarkably relaxed about the process, with very little of the stiff posed groups so common in other Victorian or Edwardian photographs.

There were many activities and events in and around the town, and the vast majority of them were preserved for posterity. Fishermen at their nets, farm workers at harvest time, shopkeepers, track-layers, coachmen and harbour workers were all captured at work, as were the folk of Campbeltown – both adults and children – going about the business of their everyday lives. The social life of the town was wide and varied, with everything from sailing, cycling and bowling to golf, picnics and walking. Parades, naval visits and proclamations were also recorded, as well as the bustling life at the quay as steamer passengers and freight were transported to and from the town.

The brothers had wide interests: both were active members of St Kieran's Church, belonged to the Volunteers (predecessors of the Territorial Army), and served as local councillors. Charles was active in the Shipwrecked Mariners Society as well as being secretary of the local branch of the Royal National Lifeboat Institution.

Their extended family were also well known in the town; their brother John and his wife Catherine established an 11-acre nursery and market garden near the then Grammar School. It had an adjacent shop with sold the produce and (much to the delight of the pupils) sweets, with their daughters Etta and Kate working there. Another daughter, Bella, worked in MacGrory's shop in Main Street in the days when (until the shop was modernised) there was still a coal fire burning behind the counter.

The brothers' photography seems to have been purely for their own interest; although a very small number of their images have appeared as postcards, it was never a commercial venture.

The result of their labours resulted in a collection of more than three thousand images stored on quarter- and half-plate negatives, stereoscopes and lantern slides. Even then their huge store of photographs might have been left neglected or, worst still, thrown out, if it hadn't been for the foresight of Charles's son A. P. MacGrory (Tony, as he was known to his many friends), who was Provost of Campbeltown between 1959 and 1964.

Tony MacGrory realised the importance of this collection, both locally and nationally, and wanted to make sure that it was accessible to the widest possible audience.

In a typically public-spirited gesture, he donated the collection to Argyll and Bute Library Service. Over a period of many years and overcoming funding restraints, the Library Service has gradually worked through the huge collection of glass plate negatives, cataloguing, printing and digitising. The one drawback to the project was that no identification of either people or places was made at the time, although local people have recently given a lot of helpful information, and many of the streets and buildings can still be recognised today. Digital images from the collection can be viewed in Campbeltown Library.

The images in this book are only a very small selection from the wonderful legacy left by Charles and Dennis MacGrory; but they give a flavour of how Campbeltown looked more than a hundred years ago – and most importantly, the people who lived and worked there.

Hampers being delivered by hand-barrow to Charles and Dennis MacGrory's shop around 1900. The shop gave the brothers an ideal vantage point to photograph events in Main Street and the Old Quay.

MacGrory Brothers Outfitters on the corner of Main Street and Bolgam Street sold everything from oilskins to fine lace. In later years the shop expanded into different departments including radios, records, sports goods and toys.

A busy scene in Main Street, with Campbeltown Cross in its original position in the middle of the road, near the Town Hall. Lloyd's Hotel can be seen in the background on the left.

A policeman is pictured in Main Street, with a large group of children lined up in the background. Shops included D. Henderson's wines and spirits as well as Stuart's tobacconist's and M. Calazel's hair salon.

James Bruce's grocer's and provision merchant, with the proprietor in the doorway and a small boy posing for the photographer, had a window display of tea at 1/6d per lb. Neighbouring shops included J. McTaggart and Paterson's watch and clock makers.

A new lifeboat, drawn by a team of horses, was paraded down Main Street past James Bruce's shop on the way to the loch, led by a member of the voluntary crew and a policeman, with a crowd of onlookers following on.

Campbeltown Cross, shown in its original position in the centre of Main Street, with the drinking fountain to serve houses without piped water. The cross was the focal point for New Year and other celebrations, with every funeral procession having to pass by it and all the Kintyre milestones measured from there. A fine example of a mediaeval Celtic cross, it was removed for safety during WWII and stored in Kilkerran cemetery. It was later re-sited near the Old Quay.

View from the top of Castlehill, with the Club, the Town Hall and the Argyll Arms Hotel, which advertised that 'Commercial gentlemen, golfers and visitors will find everything first class'. Fleming's Land on the right was built for Capt. John Fleming, one of Nelson's officers.

The same spot looking up to Castlehill, dominated by Castlehill Church which was built around 1780 to replace the Lowland Church in Kirk Street. The Sheriff Courthouse and former Free Church manses are on the right.

A carriage with its top-hatted coachman and a fine pair of greys passed the Sheriff Courthouse at Castlehill, with a crowd of people in the background. The Courthouse was built in 1871 to replace an earlier building in Bolgam Street.

Barefoot children (and a passing dog) posed for the photographers in Longrow, with a woman sitting out cleaning her windows on the right. Shop fronts just visible are Kintyre House, James McCaig, and D. McMillan, Grocer.

A view along Longrow, with a string of horses being led down the street and no motor traffic in sight. Shops in Longrow at that time included Robert Armour (plumber), John Huie (ironmonger's) and (at Mafeking Place) Daniel Mathews (furniture).

Wide Close, old Campbeltown.

The Wide Close was infamous for its squalor and poverty, with houses packed closely together, insanitary conditions, and families living in hardship. A contemporary poet summed it up: 'It was the sink of every vice, hotbed of drink and breeding lice; and slovenly crones from window sills, dumped fishes' bones and other swills.' More than sixty old flats and houses were demolished, and a new street which was described in the *Argyllshire Herald* as 'a spacious extension of our principal thoroughfare' was built in their place. After much discussion, the new street was called Longrow South.

A group of children in Longrow South, just before the road was made up. It was completed in September 1910, although a stone above Cook's Corner (site of Archie Cook's outfitter's) is dated the previous year.

Another view of the almost-complete Longrow South, looking towards Longrow. Shops on the left included D. Campbell's Kinloch Bar, and Mrs McGown's fishmonger's which had previously been in Main Street.

Union Street around 1905, running from Cross Street to Bolgam Street. The majority of the buildings on the right hand side were demolished a few years later in the construction of Longrow South.

The old Grammar School, which dates back to 1792. John and Catherine MacGrory had a market garden and sweet shop nearby. Stewart's Green in front was named after Dugald Stewart, an early rector at the Grammar.

This photograph was taken in Argyll Street, in front of the former drill hall and barracks of the Argyllshire Artillery Volunteers. The building was demolished around 1906.

An unusual view of the corner of Lorne Street and Main Street before the end tenement was demolished to make way for the Club, with the Argyll Arms Hotel being extended on to Main Street.

Deep flood water in Longrow. Planks were laid from the shop doorways to give access through the water. Flooding can still be an occasional problem here due to varying weather and tidal conditions which affect drainage.

A shop assistant at Eaglesome's anxiously watched the floods in Reform Square while small boys enjoyed the spectacle.

Flood waters were still lying in this photograph of Eaglesome's Italian Warehouse in Reform Square, with Old Highland Whisky displayed in the window. Dentist C. de Winton-Stewart had his surgery upstairs, advertising in a contemporary guidebook as 'British and American Dentistry. Established 1891. May be consulted daily on all matters appertaining to his profession. NB: I am the only qualified dentist in Campbeltown'. The Argyllshire Herald office was demolished to make way for Longrow South.

The Kintyre Agricultural Society Jubilee Show on 3rd June 1904, with a table displaying cups, trophies and rose bowls as special prizes for the best entries.

A trade stand at the Kintyre Show advertised Petol disinfectant sold at Cairnie's chemist's in Main Street. To the left was Peter MacKay's patent rick-lifter which cut out the time-consuming job of building hay on to carts.

Farm workers busy at the harvest at the Meadows Farm, near Witchburn Road, around 1900.

Women farm workers in traditional coarse sacking aprons or 'bratties', with their heads covered to protect them from the sun.

Sheep being driven up Main Street when the animals returned from winter grazing from as far afield as Ayrshire or Perthshire. They were transported by steamer, although passengers complained this left no room for them to sit in comfort.

This trade stand by a Glasgow firm at the Kintyre Show promoted an 'easy to use' nitrate fertiliser for turnips.

Pigs and other livestock were kept in many Campbeltown back yards to provide food, both to feed the family and to sell the produce to help to supplement their incomes. The shadow of the photographer – in a bowler hat – can be seen in the foreground.

Digging up the road in Hall Street in 1905 to lay the tracks for the narrow-gauge Campbeltown to Machrihanish Light Railway which opened for passengers a year later. The railway line ran along the street itself rather than on fenced-off tracks.

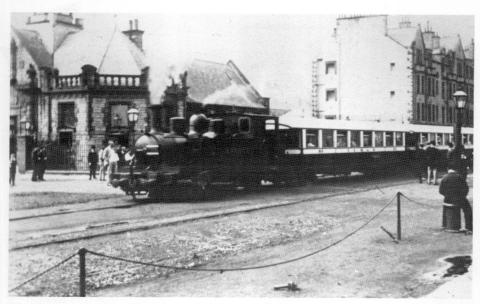

The locomotive Argyll with its distinctive passenger coaches in Hall Street with the Public Library behind. The twenty-minute journey between Campbeltown and Machrihanish cost one shilling return in 1907.

Men laying the railway tracks for the 'wee train'. The service carried 10,000 passengers in the first three weeks alone, but closed in 1932 due to the end of coal freight with the closure of the colliery, and alternative bus services for passengers.

The train is pictured passing alongside Quarry Green, before it was built up with pavements and railings. It was popular for locals and visitors alike who alighted at a small wooden station in Machrihanish behind the old Mission Hall.

The original plain Georgian façade of the White Hart Hotel before it was modernised and remodelled with its distinctive bay windows and corner tower, a process which started in 1897 and took ten years to complete.

The White Hart with its new look, advertised as having 'electric bells throughout. Telephones to Hotel Office on all landings. Boots attend all steamers'. In 1907 it cost £2 5/- for weekly board and 15/6d for the weekend.

Some local worthies stood beside the White Hart Hotel before its modernisation, on the corner of Main Street and Argyll Street.

Main Street on a quiet day in 1902, showing MacGrory's shop on the corner, with the wagon belonging to Mathews house furnishers from Mafeking Place. Edward Keith's stationer's had posters in the window advertising his opening sale.

The motor charabanc must have been a big step forward from the horse-drawn brakes. The Edwardian ladies on a day trip tied on their hats against the wind.

A newly-built skiff was pulled by hand down Main Street, accompanied by some young helpers, on its way to the loch.

The Royal Hotel was completed in 1907 after the owners of Lloyd's Hotel bought the empty adjacent site. It was advertised as 'a very handsome building which will greatly improve the amenity of the pier head'.

This view of Kirk Street shows St Kieran's Catholic School, built in 1880 with a cross on top of the centre gable, on the left. It ceased being a school in 1970.

This photograph was taken from the corner of Kirk Street and Main Street, with a hairdresser's on the left and a draper's shop with straw hats in the window.

Thomas Campbell's butcher's shop was in Kirk Street. This photograph was used in the official guide beside his advertisement: 'All meat supplied is of the best quality. Orders by post promptly attended to. Yachts, shooting lodges etc, specially catered for.'

A busy scene at the Old Quay, with the landmarks of the Christian Institute and Victoria Hall in the background.

Barochan Place in Argyll Street was designed by T. L. Watson around 1908 on the site of the old barracks. The Club can be seen in the background on the corner of Main Street.

The view from the foot of Main Street, with the Town Hall and Campbeltown Cross in the background. The Town Hall was built in 1760, when it included the town's prison cells. Its original wooden spire was rebuilt in stone in 1778.

Fisherman checking their nets on the Old Quay. Their nets were made in local net factories which were established from the mid-nineteenth century until the last one closed in 1986.

The barrels lying on the Old Quay were whisky barrels from Hazelburn distillery, stamped with the owners' names, Greenlees and Colvill. This distillery, which was one of the largest in Campbeltown, opened in 1825 and closed a hundred years later.

Fishing was one of the mainstays of the Campbeltown economy from the eighteenth century onwards, and this photo gives an indication of the huge quantities of herring landed on the pier around 1900.

Women are pictured on the Old Quay gutting the herring and packing them into barrels before they were sent to Glasgow and further afield. Many of the women travelled from fishing ports on the east of Scotland.

Campbeltown's first motor lifeboat, *William MacPherson*, was launched in 1912, serving there until replaced by the *City of Glasgow* in 1929.

The original lifeboat station was situated at the New Quay-head until a replacement was built in 1898 at the other end of Quarry Green.

Members of the RNLI lifeboat crew collected donations, with Craigdhu Mansions behind them. This was a cause well supported by the MacGrory family, and Charles MacGrory was joint secretary to the local branch of the RNLI for many years. His son Tony was local secretary for 35 years and chairman for seven years.

A fishwife dressed in her distinctive striped apron and shawl is pictured selling white fish from her hand-barrow on the Old Quay.

The herring fleet tied up at the Old Quay. The Loch Fyne skiff had a distinctive slope to its mast, which was set well forward to give the fishermen space in the middle of the boat to haul in their catch.

Skiffs drawn up for their regular spring-clean at Dalintober, with net-drying poles belonging to the fishermen seen in the background. Dalintober at this time was seen as a separate place from Campbeltown.

The Victoria Hall was built in 1887 to commemorate Queen Victoria's Golden Jubilee, as a drill hall for the Argyllshire Rifle Volunteers. The hall was rebuilt after bomb damage in WWII.

Well-dressed passengers on board the *Davaar*, one of the steamers in the Campbeltown and Glasgow Steam Packet Company along with the *Kinloch* and the *Kintyre*.

The *Davaar* ran aground on the coast of County Down in June 1895. The MacGrory brothers were two of the passengers on board, all of whom were safely rescued. The steamer was later successfully refloated.

The *Queen Alexandra*, sister ship to *King Edward* which in 1901 was the world's first turbine steamer, approaching Campbeltown quay packed with passengers.

One of many gatherings at Campbeltown Cross with the Provost and other dignitaries on the stage. This was to welcome soldiers home from the Boer War.

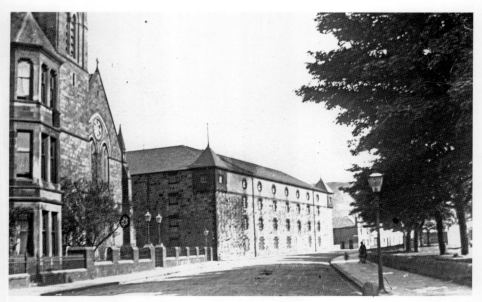

Lochhead whisky warehouse was in Lochend, just one of more than 30 distilleries which played a large part of Campbeltown's economy in the late 19th and early 20th century, producing thousands of gallons of whisky.

Robert Wylie's boatyard, with the figurehead above the door from the wreck of the clipper *Charlemagne*, wrecked on her maiden voyage in 1857. The yard, sited opposite the New Quay, built many fine skiffs.

New Quay Street looking down to the loch. The street was dominated by the Highland Parish Church built in 1807 for native Gaelic speakers, and seen in the photograph above.

The Public Library and Museum was built in 1898, designed by architect John James Burnet. It was gifted to the town by James Macalister Hall of Tangy and Killean.

Before the Campbeltown to Machrihanish Light Railway was in service, a horse-drawn brake met the steamer to take visitors for a trip to local beauty spots.

Old Quay head showing the block of old buildings which were cleared away for shops in the mid 1950s The single-storey weigh-house or 'wee'us', a popular meeting place for retired fishermen, was demolished more than thirty years ago.

A rather mischievous photo taken by the MacGrory brothers of a fellow-photographer – possibly Harold Chisholm who had his studio in Kinloch Road – with his heavy camera on a tripod on top of a cart on the Old Quay.

It was all aboard a small steam launch for a day trip to Davaar Island, with no restrictions then for health and safety requirements.

Edwardian ladies showed off the latest fashions as they took a Sunday afternoon stroll beside Campbeltown Loch.